DISCOVER
BOTTLENOSE DOLPHINS

by Virginia Loh-Hagan

Cherry Lake Publishing • Ann Arbor, Michigan

3

Published in the United States of America
by Cherry Lake Publishing
Ann Arbor, Michigan
www.cherrylakepublishing.com

Content Adviser: Karin A. Forney, Ph.D., Marine Mammal & Turtle Division, Southwest Fisheries Science Center, National Marine Fisheries Service, NOAA
Reading Adviser: Marla Conn, ReadAbility, Inc

Photo Credits: © Steve Noakes/Shutterstock Images, cover; © eZeePics Studio/Shutterstock Images, 4; © Christian Musat/Shutterstock Images, 6; © vikilikov/Shutterstock Images, 8; © anyamuse/Shutterstock Images, 10; © Willyam Bradberry/Shutterstock Images, 12; © Elena Larina/Shutterstock Images, 14; © kochkinag58/Shutterstock Images, 16; © Matt9122/ Shutterstock Images, 18; © DmitriMaruta/Shutterstock Images, 20

Library of Congress Cataloging-in-Publication Data
Loh-Hagan, Virginia, author.
  Discover bottlenose dolphins / Virginia Loh-Hagan.
      pages cm.—(Splash!)
  Summary: "This Level 3 guided reader introduces basic facts about bottlenose dolphins, including their physical characteristics, diet, and habitat. Simple callouts ask the student to think in new ways, supporting inquiry-based reading. Additional text features and search tools, including a glossary and an index, help students locate information and learn new words."— Provided by publisher.
  Audience: Ages 6–10
  Audience: K to grade 3
  Includes bibliographical references and index.
  ISBN 978-1-63362-597-6 (hardcover)—ISBN 978-1-63362-687-4 (pbk.)— ISBN 978-1-63362-777-2 (pdf)—ISBN 978-1-63362-867-0 (ebook)
  1. Bottlenose dolphin—Juvenile literature. I. Title.

QL737.C432L64 2016
599.53'3—dc23
                                    2014049845

Cherry Lake Publishing would like to acknowledge the work of the Partnership for 21st Century Skills. Please visit www.p21.org for more information.

Printed in the United States of America
Corporate Graphics

TABLE OF CONTENTS

Blubbery Mammals

Even though they live in the water, bottlenose dolphins are **mammals**. They're **warm-blooded**. They live in the cold ocean. **Blubber** keeps them warm.

Bottlenose dolphins are mammals.

They use lungs to breathe. Their nose is a **blowhole**. Every few minutes, they **surface** for air.

THINK!

Think about how the body parts of bottlenose dolphins help them live and survive in the ocean. How do they use their flippers? Why do they have pointy teeth? How does their blubber help them in a shark attack?

Blowholes are at the top of their heads.

Mothers give birth to live babies. The babies are born tail first. Mothers help babies get air. They make milk to feed their babies. The young dolphins stay with their mothers for several years.

Young dolphins stay close to their mothers.

Protective Pods

Bottlenose dolphins have long, beak-like jaws. A dolphin's lower jaws curve upward. They are longer than the upper jaws. This makes them look like they're always smiling!

Say cheese! Dolphins often seem to be smiling.

Dolphins live in **pods**. A pod can have up to 100 dolphins. The dolphins swim, hunt, and play together. They also protect one another. The dolphins separate at night when they eat. During the day, they find one another again so they can rest, play, and travel.

Dolphins stay together in pods.

They talk a lot, too! Dolphins whistle and click. Each dolphin has its own special sound. It's like they have names.

They use **echolocation** to find things. They can sense size, shape, and speed.

Bottlenose dolphins make high-pitched clicks that humans can't hear.

Quick Learners

Have you ever seen bottlenose dolphins do tricks? They learn fast. They understand commands. They can use tools, like basketballs or hula hoops.

LOOK!

Have you ever seen a bottlenose dolphin in a movie or at a show? Have you heard them whistle? Dolphins are very playful and friendly. They can teach us a lot about how to talk and work with each other. What's one way you should act more like a dolphin?

Dolphins often do tricks at water parks.

A dolphin's brain is bigger than a human's brain. The dolphin sleeps with half of its brain awake. This way, it can still breathe air and watch for **predators**.

CREATE!

Bottlenose dolphins are intelligent animals. Make a list of other intelligent animals and what makes them so smart. Rank them from most to least intelligent. Provide reasons for your rankings.

Dolphins need to watch out for predators like tiger sharks.

Tail **flukes** make dolphins great swimmers. They move their flukes up and down. Fish move their tails side to side.

There are famous stories about dolphins helping sailors by guiding boats through storms. This is not common. But people on boats often watch for these beautiful animals.

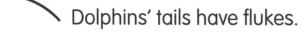

Dolphins' tails have flukes.

Think About It

Bottlenose dolphins appear in Greek myths. Find a story and read it. Why do you think people write stories about dolphins?

Dolphins' natural enemies are sharks. But humans are more dangerous to dolphins. Do you eat canned tuna? What do you think it means to eat "dolphin-safe" tuna? Learn more about how humans sometimes harm dolphins.

Ask your parents or teacher if you can visit an aquarium to see bottlenose dolphins. Before you go, write down what you think you will see. When you return home, write down what you saw.

Find Out More

BOOK
Miles, Elizabeth. *Watching Dolphins in the Ocean*. Chicago: Heinemann Library, 2006.

WEB SITE
SeaWorld Parks and Entertainment—Bottlenose Dolphins
http://seaworld.org/en/animal-info/animal-infobooks/bottlenose-dolphins/
Read in depth about many different characteristics of dolphins.

Glossary

blowhole (BLOH-hole) a hole at the top of a dolphin's head through which it breathes air

blubber (BLUHB-ur) a thick layer of fat under the dolphin's skin

echolocation (eh-koh-loh-KAY-shuhn) the ability to locate objects by producing sound waves and listening for echoes as the sound waves bounce off objects

flukes (FLOOKS) the two halves of the dolphin's tail

mammals (MAM-uhlz) animals that are warm-blooded, give birth to live babies, make milk, and breathe air

pods (PAHDZ) groups of dolphins

predators (PRED-uh-turz) animals that live by hunting other animals for food

surface (SUR-fis) to come to the top of the ocean to breathe air

warm-blooded (WORM-bluhd-id) having a warm body temperature that does not change, even if the surrounding temperature is very hot or very cold

Index

About the Author

Dr. Virginia Loh-Hagan is an author, university professor, former classroom teacher, and curriculum designer. For more than 10 years, she has been working on a very difficult cross-stich picture of dolphins. She lives in San Diego with her very tall husband and very naughty dogs. To learn more about her, visit www.virginialoh.com.